THIS BOOK
BELONGS TO:

_____

_____

_____

_____

First edition, December, 2023

Front and back cover: www.unauno.mx and Anchobee

Design and Illustrations: Anchobee

www.anchobee.com

VOL **01**

CREATIVE
THERAPHY
FOR
ANXIETY

COLORING
BOOK FOR ADULTS

Hello! I'm **ANCHOBEE**, a **PSYCHOLOGIST** and **ILLUSTRATOR** on a **MISSION** to navigate the intricate world of **MENTAL HEALTH THROUGH ART**. Raised in the vibrant chaos of an Italian family, I found solace under my bed with **BOOKS** and **COLORING PENCILS**. Coloring became my sanctuary, a **TRANSFORMATIVE PRACTICE** that **SILENCED ANXIETY** and provided an outlet for real struggles.

In my **QUEST FOR INNER PEACE**, I explored into the depths of **PSYCHOLOGY**, immersed myself in **LITERATURE**, underwent diverse **THERAPEUTIC APPROACHES**, gathered **VALUABLE INSIGHTS** from an array of podcasts and, of course, due to my own **PERSONAL EXPERIENCE** as someone living with anxiety, among other pursuits. It is from this **RICH TAPESTRY OF EXPERIENCES** that I have meticulously crafted this book.

This book is a **VISUAL VOYAGE**. Each stroke is a step towards **PEACE**, each color an **ALLY** in navigating life's **CHALLENGES**. Beyond a coloring book, it's a reflection of my experiences, inviting you to find **SOLACE** and **JOY** amidst life's ups and downs.

Join me on this journey!

HOW TO USE THIS BOOK

Welcome to your personal journey towards anxiety relief and the quest for inner peace! Here are some tips to make the most out of this mindfulness and coloring experience:

DETAILED EXPLORATION: This book is not just a coloring experience; it's a portal to emotional balance. Alongside the illustrations, you'll discover inspirational messages for you to use on this introspective journey.

REFLECTION TIME: Take the necessary time with each image and immerse yourself in reflecting on the messages left on the opposite side of each illustration. This book is an oasis of calm, a constant reminder to live in the present and find relief in every stroke of color.

THERAPEUTIC TOOL: Crafted to be more than a simple coloring book, it is a therapeutic tool to tackle anxiety. Each color, each choice, is a step towards the emotional equilibrium you seek.

COLORING TECHNIQUES: I recommend using dry techniques like colored pencils. This approach not only provides a more relaxed space for coloring but also allows for a deeper connection with each stroke.

CONSCIOUS LIGHTING: Accompany your journey with suitable lighting. A direct light will not only highlight the details of each page, but it will enhance your coloring experience and focus your mind on the present.

INSPIRATIONAL MESSAGES: Throughout the book, I've scattered messages with personal strategies that have guided me towards balance. These messages are small beacons of wisdom, intended to illuminate your own path to inner peace.

FINAL EXERCISES: Upon concluding the book, you'll discover additional exercises that I find valuable. These are small practices to strengthen your mindfulness and solidify the therapeutic benefits of this journey.

Have fun! There are no right or wrong ways to color this book. No judgment. Be free.

The opposite of fear is love.

Breathe, inhale slowly and feel your lungs fill in, then exhale and feel your lungs empty. Do this every time your mind starts to wonder, and you feel your chest tightening.

Anchobee
Bookshelf, 2023
© 2023 Anchobee / Andrea Rincon

Anxiety attack? Try math. Pick and number and multiply it by 14. Subtract 21 from the result. Divide by 6… keep it going. Your brain can't have panic mode and do math at the same time.

Plug in to life.

You can't control what other people do.

Busy hands help heal.

Find love inside you.

Other people are not your responsibility.

Love life and life will love you back.

10 minutes of sunlight a day is medicine.

Mental health is important. We all need help to navigate this sinuous road to find balance. You are not alone.

Learn to let go.

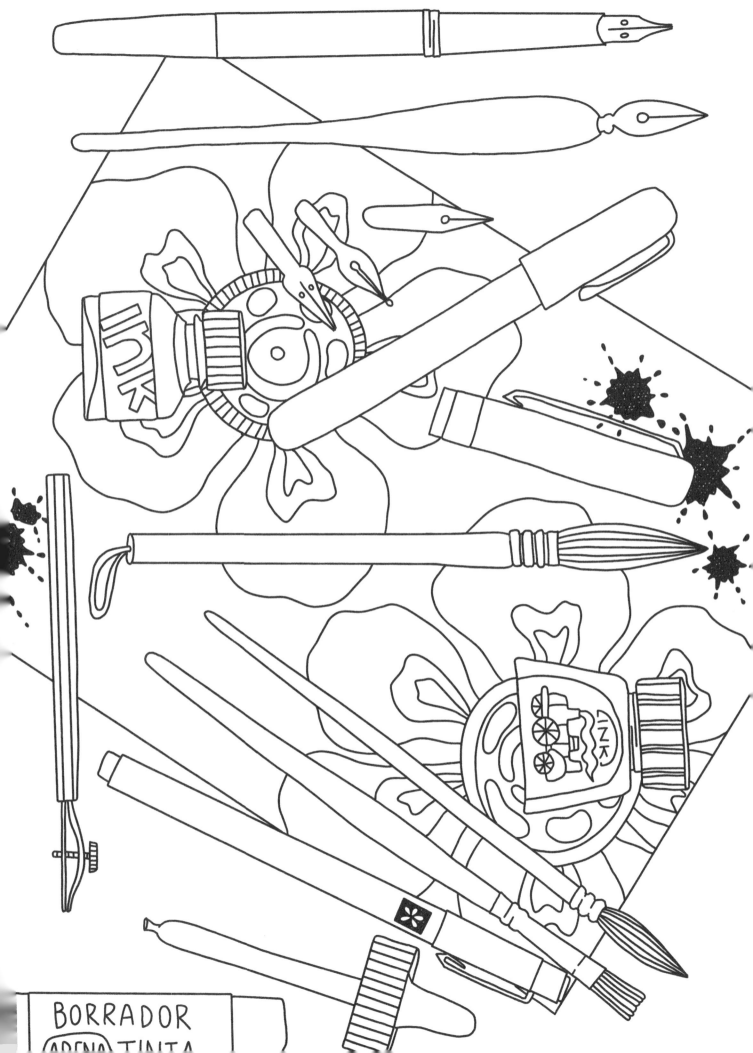

BORRADOR
TINTA

Don't assume all you hear as the truth, be selective, ask questions and question yourself.

While you color these drawings, you let your brain figure things out without the "noise" of fear and doubt.

Dream. See yourself fulfilled in the future.

The future is going to be ok.

Creativity is the ability you have to resolve issues. The more you learn the more tools you have to fill your creativity box.

Have a diary where you can express yourself freely.

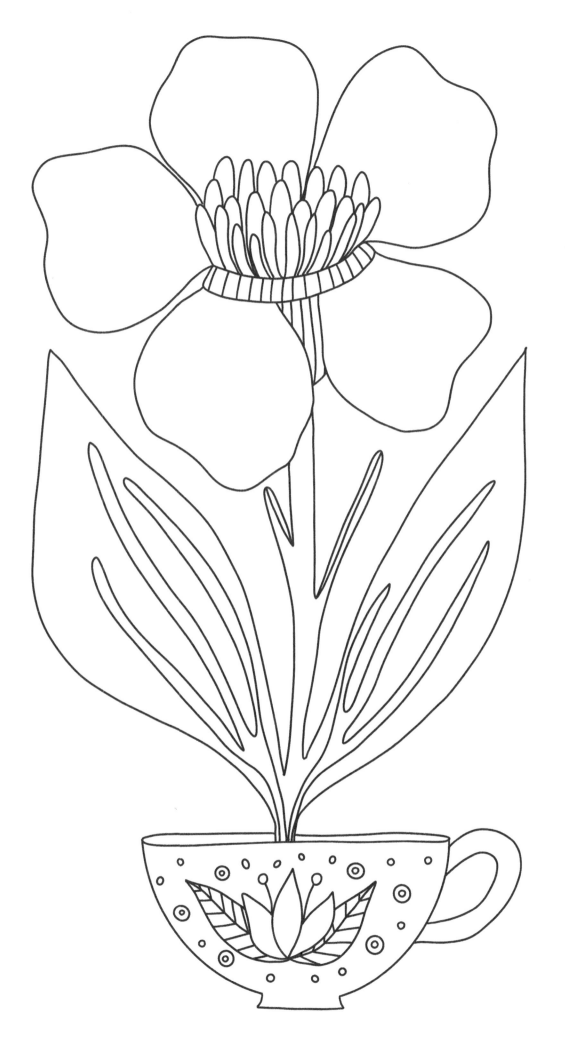

Apricity: n. the warmth of the sun in the winter.

Take one step at the time, you don't need to know what is at the end, you don't. You just need to "sense" what is the next step.

Smile when you have an anxiety attack, let your body know that everything is ok and there is no need to panic.

Being sensitive is a strength not a flaw.

Look for help. Therapists, meditation guides, the gym, doctors, friends, family…. You don't have to do this alone.

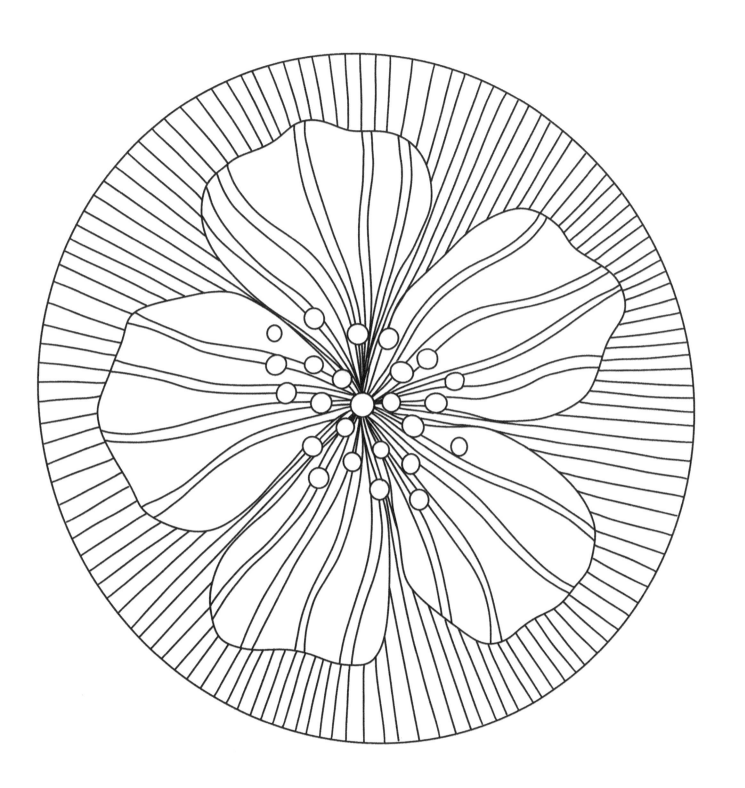

When you feel lost, literally make a new path. Take a different road to work, change your routine, make a different breakfast than the one you are used to... Change little things to open new pathways.

Panic attack? When you feel a potato stuck in your throat and you can't breathe,
1. Tell yourself you are ok, you are not dying
2. Try breathing slowly
3. Drink little sips of water
4. Cry, cry, cry
5. Once it's over, have some protein

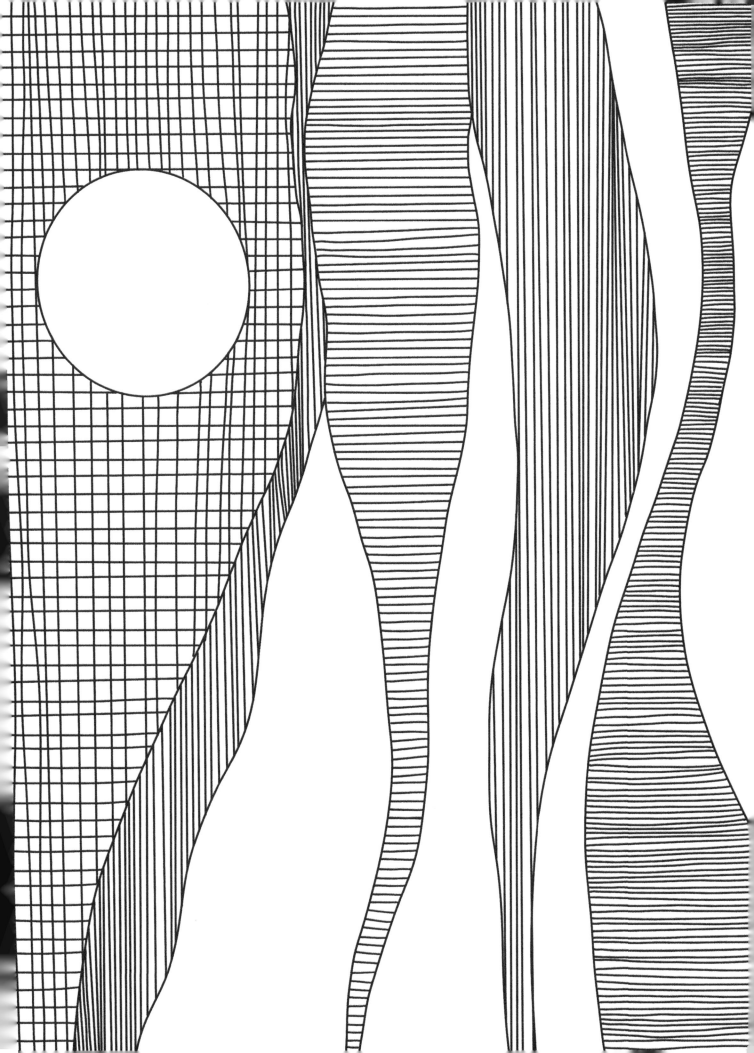

The good, the bad, the ugly, all of it makes you unique and special.

Think of a person you can call at any hour in case of emergency. Call them up an ask if you can do so.

Make a list of 10 things you love. Here is mine:
1. A nap with a cat.
2. A belly laugh, mine or someone else's.
3. The smell of damp earth.
4. A hug where I feel secure and I can let go.
5. Holding the hand of people I love.
6. How happy dogs walk.
7. A sleepy cat in the sunlight.
8. The sound of rain.
9. Grass growing on an asphalt road.
10. The spark on people's eyes when you ask them to remember a childhood smell.

Things I can't control: The actions of others, the
results of my efforts, the future, how others take care
of themselves, what other people think about me,
decisions that other people make, what happens
around me, how others react, the past, who loves me,
the opinions of others, time, the feelings of others,
what other people say.

Anchobee
Tree, 2023
© 2023 Anchobee / Andrea Rincon

Find balance inside you.

Anchobee
Summer, 2023

Things I can control: My thoughts and actions, how I talk to myself, what or who I give my energy to, my limits, how I handle challenges, what I do in my spare time, who I choose as a friend, to surrender and listen, how much time I spend doing something.

You can´t please everyone.

You may seem to be alone but you're not.

Open your eyes and absorb the beauty you see.

Set a timer to limit your screen time, especially for social media.

You are the sky, struggles are clouds. Sometimes these clouds are big and blinding and cover everything, sometimes they are little, sometimes they are big, dark and scary, but all of them will sooner or later pass. Even if you can't see the sky, the sky is always there. You are not the clouds, you are the sky.

Coloring expands your creativity.

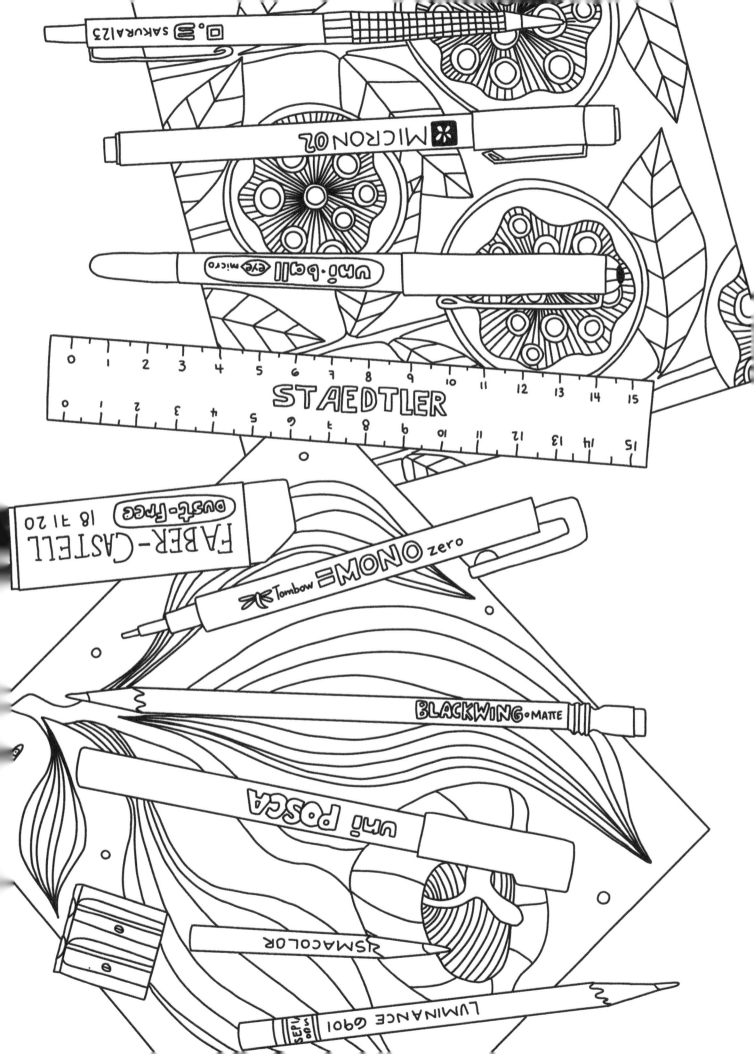

At night make a "What I Did Today" list instead of a "To Do" list.

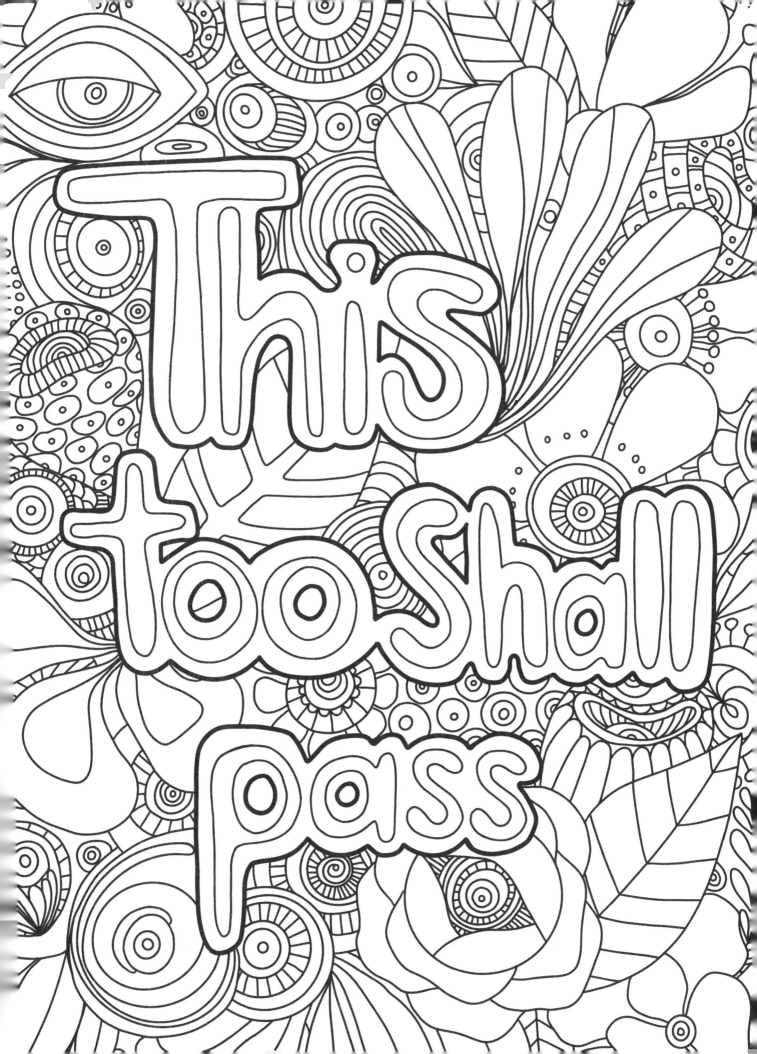

Surround yourself with life.

Choose to believe you are loved.

Forgive yourself.

Write ten things you learned about yourself while coloring this book

1.

2.

3.

4.

5.

6.

7.

8.

9.

10.

This too shall pass.

Have faith in humanity.

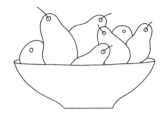

Make a list of things that makes your anxiety rise.

You are beautiful, you are part of this beautiful world, as beautiful as a tree, a plant, or a flower.

Trust your intuition.

Make a list of things that calm you down.

If you're emotionally drained, take time to regroup and find balance.

Choose what you give power to, be thorough.

Panic attack? Look around you a for elements in an increasing amount until you count to 10. For example, one computer, two cats, three lamps, four pillows .... Memorize your list, it will help you with anxiety attacks.

one

two

three

four

five

six

seven

eight

nine

ten

Always look for the positive.

USE your senses, taste something delicious, touch something pleasant, smell something that evokes good memories, look at something beautiful, listen to something that makes your soul happy.

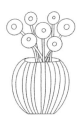

Anxiety attack? Make a list of things in alphabetical order. For example, flowers:
A Agapanthus (imagine an agapanthus), B Begonia (imagine a begonia) ...

A.

B.

C.

D.

E.

F.

G.

H.

I.

J.

K.

L.

M.

N.

P.

Q.

R.

O.

Y.

S.

U.

T.

V.

W.

X.

Z.

Social media messes with your head, be careful how much power you give it.

The best remedy for anxiety is a web of loved ones, a support system that can help you through it. If you don't have one, don't worry, find one. They don't have all to be family or friends, look for professional people around you.

Write five things the people that care about you, love about you and 5 things you love about yourself. Don't be afraid to ask. Take your time.

When you feel lost, remember other times you have felt this way. You will find the path again.

Sometimes the space within is more meaningful the thing itself.

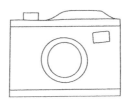

Any suggestions for my next book? Write it here and send me the pic to
coloringbook@anchobee.com

Share your coping skills with others in need.

Treat yourself and others with kindness.

You finished!
I hope you enjoyed thid book as much as I did
making it. Please give it a review and if you like
it, please recommend it to your friends.

When you forgive and let go you heal.

Try to be ok, even if people around you are not.

Acknowledgments
To my partner Luis. Holding your hand makes
everything possible, I love you.
To Calabaza and Coco. Your lovely purrs and
meows have helped me out of the darkest
places.

Love heals.

You are the adult of your inner child. Be the adult you wish you had when you were a child.

Made in the USA
Middletown, DE
14 September 2024

60843059R00060